The Agreement Book

Additional Resources from Bobbie Goodwin

The Agreement Book Series

Identity	January 2024
Wisdom	July 2024
Love	October 2024

The Agreement Book

I Agree with the Power of God Within Me

Book 2 of 4

Bobbie J. Goodwin

Authority

The Agreement Book:
   I Agree with the Power of God Within Me
Copyright © 2024 Bobbie J. Goodwin
Printed in the United States of America. All rights reserved.
ISBN-13: 9798326105530

Contents may not be reproduced in whole or in part in any form without the express written consent of the author.

Unless noted otherwise all scripture is taken from the King James Version of the Bible. Public Domain.

The Holy Bible, English Standard Version. ESV® Text Edition: 2016. Copyright © 2001 by Crossway Bibles, a publishing ministry of Good News Publishers.

Hairstylist: Faith Reed // Attire: Keeneeshia Johnson
Photography: Michael Newman
Cover Graphic: Lamont Atkins

Please Note: The content provided within this book is for general informational purposes only. The methods described within this book are the author's personal thoughts. They are not intended to be a definitive set of instructions for your life. You are responsible for any use of this material.

In honor of my Lord and Savior, Jesus,
who made everything possible

Can two walk together, except they be agreed?
—Amos 3:3

Contents

Acknowledgments	11
Introduction	15
Authority	
Week One	21
Week Two	31
Week Three	41
Week Four	51
Week Five	61
Week Six	71
Week Seven	81
Week Eight	91
Week Nine	101
Week Ten	111
Week Eleven	121
Week Twelve	131
Week Thirteen	141
About the Author	151

Acknowledgments

It is with immeasurable thankfulness that I am able to proclaim, "Thank you, Lord for another completed book!" I would like to show gratitude and appreciation to all those who stood in the gap until this book became a reality.

To the Holy Spirit, my very best friend, who never let me forget the assignment. He was always there urging and encouraging. He never allowed me to quit. I am grateful and thankful for his leadership, patience, wisdom, and endurance.

To my answered prayer, my husband, Joseph, I am forever grateful for the love and support he gave me on this journey. His prayers, financial support, time, wisdom, and encouraging talks helped me to stay motivated and see this project to completion.

Thank you to Courtney Strickland and the Next Level family for helping me to think positively and pursue my dreams.

To all my family, my three loving adult children—Arthur Jr., Joshua, and Faith, my eight blessings Nyomi, Nylani, Royalty, Bless, Joshua Jr., Princeton, Jacob, and Jeremiah. To my supportive brother (Shawn) and sister (Rochelle)—I am thankful and grateful for the belief, trust, and patience shown to me throughout this journey. I am thankful for the words of encouragement, the pushing, the love, and support that will never be forgotten.

I am most thankful for the opportunity (and ability) to share this book as part of my legacy of honoring God and my parents, the late Roosevelt and Osephine Blount. I am indebted to my parents who set the tone and laid the foundation for my life as it is today. They taught me to think for myself and make my words productive.

I would also like to thank my cousin Ella for all her prayers and encouragement, and for showing me what living for God looks like.

To Dayna Street, my college instructor at Union University. I am thankful for her insight in identifying a gift of writing in my life and suggesting that I become an author one day.

To Minister Rakesha Gray and her family. I am thankful for her time, encouraging talks, and powerful prayers to help make this dream a reality.

To Ms. Dell (STMPub.net), my talented and gifted publisher. I am thankful for her agreement to help me honor God with this book. I am so appreciative of the discussions and lunch we had at her home. I am grateful for the knowledge, time, support, and expertise she has poured into this publication.

To Apostle T. Wayne Bishop and Lady Cordia Bishop, and Minister Priscilla Griffin. I am thankful and grateful to the Lord for using them to prophesy, pray over, and deliver mighty and powerful words of encouragement into my life.

To my earthly Shepherd, Apostle A. R. Williams and to First Lady Elder Sherrilyn Williams, I could not imagine life without the knowledge and teachings they have poured into my heart. The Word of God they have taught has changed the trajectory of my life. I am forever grateful to both of them and their daughter, Trecie, who helped shape my vision.

Lastly, but definitely not least, to my "Zoom at Noon" family: Dana Williams, Mother Lucille, Minister Tina, Minister Julia, Minister Lisa T., and a host of family members and friends. I am thankful and grateful for all the revelation, love, support, wisdom, kindness, prayers, and laughter that has flowed through the airwaves from the website.

I am especially grateful to Dana Williams for agreeing with God to carry out the assignment of honoring God during her lunch break.

Introduction

Dark clouds, heavy rain, tumultuous winds, trees swaying and falling, heavy objects being carried from one location to the next, thundering, and flashes of lightning—all of these are signs and proof that God's power is more real than can be measured by man. These are all signs of a storm, tornado, hurricane, or some other unfavorable weather pattern. Just as storms happen within the earth, with a power that cannot be matched, so is the power within believers of Jesus Christ.

When we talk about power and/or authority we cannot discuss it with clarity and understanding without discussing its origin. **God is the source of all power**. He is all powerful. His son, Jesus, came into the earth to set the example for us to live, using his father's power.

After he was hanged, crucified, and buried, he was also resurrected. Jesus now sits on the righthand side of the Father, with all power in his hands. When he ascended into heaven, he left his spirit here on the earth as an opportunity to obtain power. It is readily available to all who will ask and receive it. His Spirit is holy, righteous, and pure.

The Holy Spirit is where we get our power which causes us to do the will of God. Performing the will of the Father is whole reason for being in the earth. This is why we, as believers, have power—not to perform our will but to do the will of him who sent us.

We must know and understand, not only who we are, but also what we have been given the authority to do. God has delegated his authority and power to all believers of Jesus Christ. This book will help you know the source of your power and authority. It will also help you renew your mind to walk in divine power, defeat the enemy, and take back your life of fulfilling the will of the Father on the earth.

Agreements occur everywhere in our lives. We make agreements knowingly and unknowingly. Whether you realize it or not, you made an agreement when you accepted this book. If you purchased it, then money was exchanged, and you received the book. If it was given to you, then you chose to receive it. Now that you are reading the book, you are making an agreement to allow the content of this book to impact your thinking.

An agreement can be defined in many ways. To keep it simple, I will define it as an action for an action. Any agreement requires action from all parties. Everyone must take action to move in the same direction as the terms of what is being offered or said.

The Bible says, "If you confess with your mouth that Jesus is Lord and believe in your heart that God raised him from the dead, you will be saved. For with the heart, one believes and is justified, and with the mouth one confesses and is saved" (Romans 10:9–10 ESV).

This is the greatest agreement you can ever make in your entire life! Your greatest life begins when you take action by agreeing with God for your salvation.

Making that confession grants authority. The purpose of this book is to bring you into agreement with your new, God-given authority in Christ, and about agreeing with the power of God within you.

For the next 13 weeks, you will have the opportunity to agree with 91 devotionals about the power and authority you have as a believer.

God has already given his Word, his Son, and his Spirit as a testimony of who *He* is and who *we* are. Those were *his* actions. Now, we have to agree with those actions and take action by accepting, believing, and following the Word of God.

With each devotional, read the scripture, acknowledge it in your heart, speak it out your mouth, and check it on the page as an act of agreement.

Each week, you will be presented with what I like to call, "Heroes of Power." God enabled these men and women to do mighty works.

One of the most well-known heroes of faith and power is David. He is best known for his encounter with Goliath. You may never have a physical encounter with a 9-ft. giant-human warrior, but there have been, there are, or may be times when you deal with giant-size issues. These issues may involve family, other relationships, finances, health, or even spiritual matters.

Another Hero of Power is Joshua. He used the authority of divine, strategic leadership to bring down the walls of Jericho (Joshua 6). What was God's purpose behind it? It was to show the people that God's plans of victory are always better than human plans.

Just as God gave power to these heroes, the same God can and will give you the power and authority to carry out His plan. These weren't special people. They began their journey like ordinary people—just like you and me.

Believe that God has already authorized His children to be heroes of power. Believe it. Claim it. Stand on it. Take authority!

Agree with the power of God that is within you!

Week One

Hero of Power: Jesus	23
Day 1: The First Thing God Gave Us was Power (Dominion)	24
Day 2: God Gave Us Power to Have His Nature and Character	25
Day 3: God Gave Us the Power to be Blessed as a Male and Female Unit	26
Day 4: We Have Been Given the Power to Have Food Provision for Our Bodies	27
Day 5: God Has Given the Power of Choice to be Saved Through His Son Jesus	28
Day 6: God Gives Us the Power to Receive His Breath of Life	29
Day 7: God Will Allow Us to See Our Enemies Defeated and Flee From Us Seven Different Ways	30

Hero of Power: Jesus

Power/Authority:
Jesus used his authority and obedience from conception until resurrection to do the will of the Father.

Purpose/Why:
So that everyone who believes will have an opportunity for salvation and return to the only true and living God and live eternally (John 3:16–18).

Do you agree this power and/or authority is still actively available for use today?

| ☐ I agree | ☐ I disagree | ☐ I'm working on it |

The First Thing God Gave Us was Power (Dominion)

Let us make man in our image, after our likeness. And let them have dominion over the fish of the sea and over the birds of the heavens and over the livestock and over all the earth and over every creeping thing that creeps on the earth.

—Genesis 1:26 ESV

Daily Agreement:
I agree that God gave me power as a priority to care for and rule over all he created.

| ☐ I agree | ☐ I disagree | ☐ I'm working on it |

God Gave Us Power to Have His Nature and Character

So God created man in his own image, in the image of God he created him; male and female he created them.
—Genesis 1:27 ESV

Daily Agreement:
I agree, I have authority to mirror God.

| ☐ I agree | ☐ I disagree | ☐ I'm working on it |

God Gave Us the Power to be Blessed as a Male and Female Unit

And God blessed them. And God said to them, "Be fruitful and multiply and fill the earth and subdue it and have dominion over the fish of the sea and over the birds of the heavens and over every living thing that moves on the earth."

—Genesis 1:28 ESV

Daily Agreement:
I agree that with the union of male and female, we have the power to reproduce, multiply, replenish, and subdue the earth.

| ☐ I agree | ☐ I disagree | ☐ I'm working on it |

We Have Been Given the Power to Have Food Provision for Our Bodies

And God said, Behold, I have given you every herb bearing seed, which is upon the face of all the earth, and every tree, in the which is the fruit of a tree yielding seed; to you it shall be for meat.

—Genesis 1:29 ESV

Daily Agreement:
I agree that God gave us the power to obtain herbs and fruits from every tree from all the earth as meat.

| ☐ I agree | ☐ I disagree | ☐ I'm working on it |

God Has Given the Power of Choice to be Saved Through His Son Jesus

"For God so loved the world, that he gave his only Son, that whoever believes in him should not perish but have eternal life. For God did not send his Son into the world to condemn the world, but in order that the world might be saved through him. Whoever believes in him is not condemned, but whoever does not believe is condemned already, because he has not believed in the name of the only Son of God…"

—John 3:16–18 ESV

Daily Agreement:
I agree, I have been given the power of choice to be saved or to be condemned.

☐ I agree	☐ I disagree	☐ I'm working on it

God Gives Us the Power to Receive His Breath of Life

The LORD God formed the man of dust from the ground and breathed into his nostrils the breath of life, and the man became a living creature.

—Genesis 2:7 ESV

Daily Agreement:
I agree God gives me the power to be a living creature with his breath of life on the inside of me.

| ☐ I agree | ☐ I disagree | ☐ I'm working on it |

God Will Allow Us to See Our Enemies Defeated and Flee From Us Seven Different Ways

"The Lord will cause your enemies who rise against you to be defeated before you. They shall come out against you one way and flee before you seven ways."
—Deuteronomy 28:7 ESV

Daily Agreement:
I agree by God's authority, my enemies will flee from me seven different ways.

| ☐ I agree | ☐ I disagree | ☐ I'm working on it |

Week Two

Hero of Power: Jeremiah	33
Day 1: Through Jesus I Have Authority Over All the Power of the Enemy	34
Day 2: The Holy Spirit Allows Me to Receive Power to be a Witness of Jesus	35
Day 3: Our Father Will Empower Us to Speak Without Hesitation	36
Day 4: All Authority was Given to Jesus—He Delegated His Power to Us to Make Disciples of Him	37
Day 5: As a Believer, I Have the Power to Cast Out Devils and Speak with New Tongues	38
Day 6: God Has Empowered Us with All Spiritual Blessings	39
Day 7: We Have the Authority to be Seated in Heavenly Places in Christ Jesus	40

Hero of Power: Jeremiah

Power/Authority:

Before Jeremiah was born, he was purposed to use the power of prophecy to declare the judgement of God in response to unrepented wickedness (Jeremiah 1:5–17).

Purpose/Why:

Jeremiah was God's chosen mouthpiece to deliver His word to the people for that time period.

Do you agree this power and/or authority is still actively available for use today?

| ☐ I agree | ☐ I disagree | ☐ I'm working on it |

Through Jesus I Have Authority Over All the Power of the Enemy

Behold, I have given you authority to tread on serpents and scorpions, and over all the power of the enemy, and nothing shall hurt you.

—Luke 10:19 ESV

Daily Agreement:
I agree, nothing shall hurt me because Jesus gives me all authority and power over the enemy.

| ☐ I agree | ☐ I disagree | ☐ I'm working on it |

The Holy Spirit Allows Me to Receive Power to be a Witness of Jesus

"… But you will receive power when the Holy Spirit has come upon you, and you will be my witnesses in Jerusalem and in all Judea and Samaria, and to the end of the earth."

—Acts 1:8 ESV

Daily Agreement:
I agree that once I receive the Holy Spirit, I will have the power to witness about Jesus until the end of the earth.

| ☐ I agree | ☐ I disagree | ☐ I'm working on it |

Our Father Will Empower Us to Speak Without Hesitation

When they deliver you over, do not be anxious about how you are to speak or what you are to say, for what you are to say will be given to you in that hour. For it is not you who speak, but the Spirit of your Father speaking through you.

—Matthew 10:19–20 ESV

Daily Agreement:
I agree, I do not have to worry about what to say because the Spirit of my Father will speak through me.

☐ I agree	☐ I disagree	☐ I'm working on it

All Authority was Given to Jesus—He Delegated His Power to Us to Make Disciples of Him

And Jesus came and said to them, "All authority in heaven and on earth has been given to me. Go therefore and make disciples of all nations, baptizing them in the name of the Father and of the Son and of the Holy Spirit, teaching them to observe all that I have commanded you. And behold, I am with you always, to the end of the age."

—Matthew 28:18–20 ESV

Daily Agreement:

I agree that as a believer in Jesus, I have the authority to make disciples and teach them to do all that Jesus commands.

| ☐ I agree | ☐ I disagree | ☐ I'm working on it |

As a Believer, I Have the Power to Cast Out Devils and Speak with New Tongues

And these signs shall follow them that believe; In my name shall they cast out devils; they shall speak with new tongues.
—Mark 16:17

Daily Agreement:
I agree, I have the power to cast out devils and speak with new tongues as a believer in Jesus Christ.

| ☐ I agree | ☐ I disagree | ☐ I'm working on it |

God Has Empowered Us with All Spiritual Blessings

Blessed be the God and Father of our Lord Jesus Christ, who hath blessed us with all spiritual blessings in heavenly places in Christ:

—Ephesians 1:3

Daily Agreement:
I agree and receive all spiritual blessings from God, the Father of Jesus.

| ☐ I agree | ☐ I disagree | ☐ I'm working on it |

We Have the Authority to be Seated in Heavenly Places in Christ Jesus

Even when we were dead in sins, hath quickened us together with Christ, (by grace ye are saved;) And hath raised us up together, and made us sit together in heavenly places in Christ Jesus.

—Ephesians 2:5–6

Daily Agreement:
I agree, I am saved by grace and seated in heavenly places with Christ Jesus.

| ☐ I agree | ☐ I disagree | ☐ I'm working on it |

Week Three

Hero of Power: Jacob	43
Day 1: I Have Been Given Power to Get Wealth	44
Day 2: God Has All Power	45
Day 3: God Gives Power to His People	46
Day 4: I Have Permission to Wait Beside the Lord as He Makes My Enemies My Footstool	47
Day 5: I Have Power in My Tongue to Speak Death or Life	48
Day 6: God Gives Me Power Even When I Feel Faint and Have No Strength	49
Day 7: As a Disciple of Jesus, I Have Power to Heal All Sickness and Diseases	50

Hero of Power: Jacob

Power/Authority:

Jacob used strength and determination to wrestle with God and man and did overcome (Genesis 32:24–32).

Purpose/Why:

To get the blessing he desired—the result was his name was changed from Jacob to Israel. Jacob saw God face to face, yet his life was spared.

Do you agree this power and/or authority is still actively available for use today?

| ☐ I agree | ☐ I disagree | ☐ I'm working on it |

I Have Been Given Power to Get Wealth

But thou shalt remember the Lord thy God: for it is he that giveth thee power to get wealth, that he may establish his covenant which he swore unto thy fathers, as it is this day.
—Deuteronomy 8:18

Daily Agreement:
I agree, God gives me power to get wealth to establish his covenant.

☐ I agree   ☐ I disagree   ☐ I'm working on it

God Has All Power

God hath spoken once; twice have I heard this; that power belongs unto God. Also unto thee, O Lord, belongs mercy: for thou render to every man according to his work.

—Psalm 62:11–12

Daily Agreement:
I agree, God has all power and gives every man according to his work.

| ☐ I agree | ☐ I disagree | ☐ I'm working on it |

God Gives Power to His People

O God, thou art terrible out of thy holy places: the God of Israel is he that giveth strength and power unto his people. Blessed be God.

—Psalm 68:35

Daily Agreement:
I agree, God gives power to his people!

| ☐ I agree | ☐ I disagree | ☐ I'm working on it |

I Have Permission to Wait Beside the Lord as He Makes My Enemies My Footstool

The Lord said unto my Lord, sit thou at my right hand, until I make thine enemies thy footstool.

—Psalm 110:1

Daily Agreement:
I agree, as I sit with the Lord, he will make my enemies my footstool.

| ☐ I agree | ☐ I disagree | ☐ I'm working on it |

I Have Power in My Tongue to Speak Death or Life

Death and life are in the power of the tongue: and they that love it shall eat the fruit thereof.

—Proverbs 18:21

Daily Agreement:
I agree, I use the power in my tongue to speak life.

| ☐ I agree | ☐ I disagree | ☐ I'm working on it |

God Gives Me Power Even When I Feel Faint and Have No Strength

He giveth power to the faint; and to them that have no might he increases strength.

—Isaish 40:29

Daily Agreement:
I agree, the Lord increases my strength even when I feel I have no power.

| ☐ I agree | ☐ I disagree | ☐ I'm working on it |

As a Disciple of Jesus, I Have Power to Heal All Sickness and Diseases

And when he had called unto him his twelve disciples, he gave them power against unclean spirits, to cast them out, and to heal all manner of sickness and all manner of disease.
—Matthew 10:1

Daily Agreement:
I agree through the power given to me from Jesus, I can cast out unclean spirits and heal sickness and diseases.

| ☐ I agree | ☐ I disagree | ☐ I'm working on it |

Week Four

Hero of Power: Moses	53
Day 1: As a Disciple of Jesus, I Have Power and Authority Over All Devils	54
Day 2: I Believe and Receive the Power to Become a Son or Daughter of God	55
Day 3: I Believe the Gospel of Christ is the Power of God Unto Salvation	56
Day 4: I Have Dominion Over the Works of My Hands	57
Day 5: I Will Abound in Hope Through the Power of the Holy Spirit	58
Day 6: The Power that Works Within Me Does More than I Can Think or Imagine	59
Day 7: God Has Given Me Power, Love, and a Strong Mind	60

Hero of Power: Moses

Power/Authority:

Moses used the power of a personal relationship with God to access places that others were not allowed to enter (Exodus 24:2).

Purpose/Why:

Through Moses' intimate relationship with God, Moses obtained the tables of stone with the law and the commandments which God had written and told Moses to teach them.

Do you agree this power and/or authority is still actively available for use today?

| ☐ I agree | ☐ I disagree | ☐ I'm working on it |

As a Disciple of Jesus, I Have Power and Authority Over All Devils

Then he called his twelve disciples together, and gave them power and authority over all devils, and to cure diseases.

—Luke 9:1

Daily Agreement:
I agree through the power given to me from Jesus, I have power and authority of all devils.

| ☐ I agree | ☐ I disagree | ☐ I'm working on it |

I Believe and Receive the Power to Become a Son or Daughter of God

But as many as received him, to them gave the power to become the sons of God, even to them that believe on his name: Which were born, not of blood, nor of the will of the flesh, nor of the will of man, but of God.

—John 1:12–13

Daily Agreement:
I agree, I have the power to be a son/daughter of God.

| ☐ I agree | ☐ I disagree | ☐ I'm working on it |

I Believe the Gospel of Christ is the Power of God Unto Salvation

For I am not ashamed of the gospel of Christ: for it is the power of God unto salvation to everyone that believeth; to the Jew first, and also to the Greek.

—Romans 1:16

Daily Agreement:
I agree that I am not ashamed, but I receive the power of God unto salvation.

| ☐ I agree | ☐ I disagree | ☐ I'm working on it |

I Have Dominion Over the Works of My Hands

You have given him dominion over the works of your hands; you have put all things under his feet.

—Psalm 8:6 ESV

Daily Agreement:
I agree by the authority of God, I have power over my hands. All things are under my feet.

| ☐ I agree | ☐ I disagree | ☐ I'm working on it |

I Will Abound in Hope Through the Power of the Holy Spirit

Now the God of hope fill you with all joy and peace in believing, that ye may abound in hope, through the power of the Holy Ghost.

—Romans 15:13

Daily Agreement:
I agree that I believe the God of hope will fill me with joy and peace through the power of the Holy Ghost.

| ☐ I agree | ☐ I disagree | ☐ I'm working on it |

The Power that Works Within Me Does More than I Can Think or Imagine

Now unto him that is able to do exceeding abundantly above all that we ask or think, according to the power that worketh in us.

—Ephesians 3:20

Daily Agreement:
I agree that the power working within me goes beyond what I can ask or think.

| ☐ I agree | ☐ I disagree | ☐ I'm working on it |

God Has Given Me Power, Love, and a Strong Mind

For God hath not given us the spirit of fear; but of power, and of love, and of a sound mind.

—2 Timothy 1:7

Daily Agreement:
I agree, I have power, love, and a strong mind.

☐ I agree	☐ I disagree	☐ I'm working on it

Week Five

Hero of Power: Daniel	63
Day 1: The Power of Submission Unto God and Resisting the Devil, Makes the Devil Flee from You	64
Day 2: When You Please the Lord, Even Your Enemies Will be at Peace with You	65
Day 3: The Holy Spirit Will Allow You to Remember All that God Has Told You	66
Day 4: The Power of the Blood of Jesus Provides Eternal Redemption	67
Day 5: The Power of Faith Will Move Mountains	68
Day 6: The Power of Praying in the Holy Ghost Builds Your Most Holy Faith	69
Day 7: The Power of God Will Keep Me From Falling	70

Hero of Power: Daniel

Power/Authority:

In many instances throughout the Bible, Daniel used the power of vision to carry out the will of God (Daniel 10:7–8).

Purpose/Why:

To interpret the revelation of God to the people in the earth.

Do you agree this power and/or authority is still actively available for use today?

| ☐ I agree | ☐ I disagree | ☐ I'm working on it |

The Power of Submission Unto God and Resisting the Devil, Makes the Devil Flee from You

Submit yourselves therefore to God. Resist the devil, and he will flee from you.

—James 4:7

Daily Agreement:
I agree, when I submit to the Lord and resist the devil, then the devil will run from me.

| ☐ I agree | ☐ I disagree | ☐ I'm working on it |

When You Please the Lord, Even Your Enemies Will be at Peace with You

When a man's ways please the Lord, he maketh even his enemies to be at peace with him.

—Proverbs 16:7

Daily Agreement:
I agree, when my ways are pleasing to the Lord, he brings my enemies into peace with me.

| ☐ I agree | ☐ I disagree | ☐ I'm working on it |

The Holy Spirit Will Allow You to Remember All that God Has Told You

But the Comforter, which is the Holy Ghost, whom the Father will send in my name, he shall teach you all things, and bring all things to your remembrance, whatsoever I have said unto you.

—John 14:26

Daily Agreement:
I agree, the Holy Spirit teaches me all things and reminds me of what God said.

| ☐ I agree | ☐ I disagree | ☐ I'm working on it |

The Power of the Blood of Jesus Provides Eternal Redemption

Neither by the blood of goats and calves, but by his own blood he entered in once into the holy place, having obtained eternal redemption for us.

—Hebrews 9:12

Daily Agreement:
I agree, Jesus' blood has redeemed me.

| ☐ I agree | ☐ I disagree | ☐ I'm working on it |

The Power of Faith Will Move Mountains

For verily I say unto you, that whosoever shall say unto this mountain, Be thou removed, and be thou cast into the sea; and shall not doubt in his heart but shall believe that those things which he saith shall come to pass; he shall have whatsoever he saith.

—Mark 11:23

Daily Agreement:
I agree, if I tell the mountain in my life to be moved, and do not doubt, it shall be moved.

| ☐ I agree | ☐ I disagree | ☐ I'm working on it |

The Power of Praying in the Holy Ghost Builds Your Most Holy Faith

But ye, beloved, building up yourselves on your most holy faith, praying in the Holy Ghost.

—Jude 1:20

Daily Agreement:
I agree, praying in the Holy Ghost builds up my most holy faith.

| ☐ I agree | ☐ I disagree | ☐ I'm working on it |

The Power of God Will Keep Me From Falling

Now unto him that is able to keep you from falling, and to present you faultless before the presence of his glory with exceeding joy, to the only wise God our Saviour, be glory and majesty, dominion, and power, both now and ever. Amen.

—Jude 1:24–25

Daily Agreement:
I agree that the only wise God, my Savior, can keep me from falling and present me faultless in his presence with exceeding joy.

| ☐ I agree | ☐ I disagree | ☐ I'm working on it |

Week Six

Hero of Power: Peter	73
Day 1: All Things are Possible with God	74
Day 2: Jesus is All Powerful in Heaven and Earth	75
Day 3: The Power of Believing When You Pray Causes You to Receive What You Pray For	76
Day 4: The Eternal Power of the Reward of Following Jesus	77
Day 5: With the Strength of God, I Can Do All Things	78
Day 6: As a Believer of Jesus, I Have the Power to Hear and Believe the Word of God and Have Everlasting Life	79
Day 7: Obey the Lord and His Commandments and Be Empowered	80

Hero of Power: Peter

Power/Authority:
Peter used the power of healing to carry out the will of God (Acts 3:3–8).

Purpose/Why:
To bring praise, glory and honor to God for all he has done.

Do you agree this power and/or authority is still actively available for use today?

| ☐ I agree | ☐ I disagree | ☐ I'm working on it |

All Things are Possible with God

For with God nothing shall be impossible.

—Luke 1:37

Daily Agreement:
I agree with God that everything is possible.

| ☐ I agree | ☐ I disagree | ☐ I'm working on it |

Jesus is All Powerful in Heaven and Earth

And Jesus came and spake unto them, saying, all power is given unto me in heaven and in earth.

—Matthew 28:18

Daily Agreement:
I agree, Jesus has all power in heaven and earth.

| ☐ I agree | ☐ I disagree | ☐ I'm working on it |

The Power of Believing When You Pray Causes You to Receive What You Pray For

And all things, whatsoever ye shall ask in prayer, believing, ye shall receive.

—Matthew 21:22

Daily Agreement:
I agree, I believe when I pray therefore I receive.

| ☐ I agree | ☐ I disagree | ☐ I'm working on it |

The Eternal Power of the Reward of Following Jesus

Then answered Peter and said unto him, behold, we have forsaken all, and followed thee; what shall we have therefore? And Jesus said unto them, Verily I say unto you, that ye which have followed me, in the regeneration when the Son of man shall sit in the throne of his glory, ye also shall sit upon twelve thrones, judging the twelve tribes of Israel. And everyone that hath forsaken houses, or brethren, or sisters, or father, or mother, or wife, or children, or lands, for my name's sake, shall receive an hundredfold, and shall inherit everlasting life

—Matthew 19:27–29

Daily Agreement:

I agree to follow Jesus and receive eternal power as a reward of following Jesus.

| ☐ I agree | ☐ I disagree | ☐ I'm working on it |

With the Strength of God, I Can Do All Things

I can do all things through Christ which strengtheneth me.
—Philippians 4:13

Daily Agreement:
I agree, I can do anything with the strength of Christ.

| ☐ I agree | ☐ I disagree | ☐ I'm working on it |

As a Believer of Jesus, I Have the Power to Hear and Believe the Word of God and Have Everlasting Life

Truly, truly, I say to you, whoever hears my word and believes him who sent me has eternal life. He does not come into judgment, but has passed from death to life.
—John 5:24 ESV

Daily Agreement:
I agree to hear and believe in Him who sent Jesus; therefore, I have eternal life.

| ☐ I agree | ☐ I disagree | ☐ I'm working on it |

Obey the Lord and His Commandments and Be Empowered

Now this is the commandment—the statutes and the rules—that the Lord your God commanded me to teach you, that you may do them in the land to which you are going over, to possess it, that you may fear the Lord your God, you and your son and your son's son, by keeping all his statutes and his commandments, which I command you, all the days of your life, and that your days may be long. Hear therefore, O Israel, and be careful to do them, that it may go well with you, and that you may multiply greatly, as the Lord, the God of your fathers, has promised you, in a land flowing with milk and honey.

—Deuteronomy 6:1–3 ESV

Daily Agreement:
I agree, when I obey the commandments of the Lord, my life is empowered to multiply and prosper.

☐ I agree	☐ I disagree	☐ I'm working on it

Week Seven

Hero of Power: Paul   83
Day 1: For Those of Us Who Have Authority,
   We Should Also Lead Quiet, Peaceful, Honest,
   and Godly Lives   84
Day 2: As Saints of the Lord, We Have the Authority
   to Experience No Want in Our Lives   85
Day 3: The Righteous Has Authority to Receive
   Deliverance from All Afflictions   86
Day 4: I Have the Authority to Use the Word of God
   to Speak to Angels   87
Day 5: I Have the Authority to Prosper
   as My Soul Prospers   88
Day 6: The Power of the Blood of Jesus
   Cleanses Me from All Sin   89
Day 7: The Power of the Blood of Jesus Justifies Me   90

Hero of Power: Paul

Power/Authority:
Paul used the power of the Holy Spirit to write the majority of the New Testament scriptures.

Purpose/Why:
To share the gospel of Jesus Christ with the people in the earth.

Do you agree this power and/or authority is still actively available for use today?

| ☐ I agree | ☐ I disagree | ☐ I'm working on it |

For Those of Us Who Have Authority, We Should Also Lead Quiet, Peaceful, Honest, and Godly Lives

For kings, and for all that are in authority; that we may lead a quiet and peaceable life in all godliness and honesty. For this is good and acceptable in the sight of God our Saviour.
—1 Timothy 2:2–3

Daily Agreement:
I agree, as I continue in authority, I will lead a life that is acceptable in the sight of the Lord.

☐ I agree   ☐ I disagree   ☐ I'm working on it

As Saints of the Lord, We Have the Authority to Experience No Want in Our Lives

O fear the Lord, ye his saints: for there is no want to them that fear him.

—Psalm 34:9

Daily Agreement:
I agree, when I fear the Lord, there is no want in my life.

| ☐ I agree | ☐ I disagree | ☐ I'm working on it |

The Righteous Has Authority to Receive Deliverance from All Afflictions

Many are the afflictions of the righteous, but the Lord delivers him out of them all.

—Psalm 34:19 ESV

Daily Agreement:
I agree, I am righteous through Jesus Christ, therefore I am delivered from all afflictions.

| ☐ I agree | ☐ I disagree | ☐ I'm working on it |

I Have the Authority to Use the Word of God to Speak to Angels

Bless the Lord, ye his angels, that excel in strength, that do his commandments, hearkening unto the voice of his word.
—Psalm 103:20

Daily Agreement:
I agree that when I speak the Word of God to angels, they are listening to do as the Lord commands.

| ☐ I agree | ☐ I disagree | ☐ I'm working on it |

I Have the Authority to Prosper as My Soul Prospers

Beloved, I wish above all things that thou mayest prosper and be in health, even as thy soul prospereth.

—3 John 2

Daily Agreement:
I agree, I am in health and prosper as my soul prospers.

☐ I agree ☐ I disagree ☐ I'm working on it

The Power of the Blood of Jesus Cleanses Me from All Sin

But if we walk in the light, as he is in the light, we have fellowship one with another, and the blood of Jesus Christ his Son cleanseth us from all sin.

—1 John 1:7

Daily Agreement:
I agree, the power of the blood of Jesus cleanses me from all sin.

| ☐ I agree | ☐ I disagree | ☐ I'm working on it |

The Power of the Blood of Jesus Justifies Me

Much more then, being now justified by his blood, we shall be saved from wrath through him.

—Romans 5:9

Daily Agreement:
I agree that through the power of the blood of Jesus, I am justified.

☐ I agree ☐ I disagree ☐ I'm working on it

Week Eight

Heroine of Power: Esther — 93
Day 1: The Blood Has Protection Power for My House — 94
Day 2: The Power of the Blood of Christ Redeemed Me from My Past — 95
Day 3: The Power of the Blood of Jesus Grants Entry into the Holiest — 96
Day 4: Through the Power of the Blood of Christ My Conscience is Free from Dead Works — 97
Day 5: By the Power of the Stripes of Jesus I am Healed — 98
Day 6: Using the Word of God is Powerful— It is Sharper than Any Double-Edge Sword — 99
Day 7: Through God's Divine Power, I Have All Things Pertaining to Life and Godliness — 100

Heroine of Power: Esther

Power/Authority:
Esther used the power of prayer and fasting to honor God (Esther 4:15–16).

Purpose/Why:
To prove that God can overturn evil plots and provide freedom for families.

Do you agree this power and/or authority is still actively available for use today?

| ☐ I agree | ☐ I disagree | ☐ I'm working on it |

The Blood Has Protection Power for My House

And the blood shall be to you for a token upon the houses where ye are: and when I see the blood, I will pass over you, and the plague shall not be upon you to destroy you, when I smite the land of Egypt.

— Exodus 12:13

Daily Agreement:
I agree, the power of the blood protects my home.

| ☐ I agree | ☐ I disagree | ☐ I'm working on it |

The Power of the Blood of Christ Redeemed Me from My Past

Forasmuch as ye know that ye were not redeemed with corruptible things, as silver and gold, from your vain conversation received by tradition from your fathers; but with the precious blood of Christ, as of a lamb without blemish and without spot.

—1 Peter 1:18–19

Daily Agreement:
I agree, the blood of Jesus is my redemption power.

| ☐ I agree | ☐ I disagree | ☐ I'm working on it |

The Power of the Blood of Jesus Grants Entry into the Holiest

Having therefore, brethren, boldness to enter into the holiest by the blood of Jesus.

—Hebrews 10:19

Daily Agreement:
I agree, I can worship in the holiest by the power of the blood of Jesus.

| ☐ I agree | ☐ I disagree | ☐ I'm working on it |

Through the Power of the Blood of Christ My Conscience is Free from Dead Works

How much more shall the blood of Christ, who through the eternal Spirit offered himself without spot to God, purge your conscience from dead works to serve the living God?
—Hebrews 9:14 ESV

Daily Agreement:
I agree, the power of the blood of Jesus cleans my mind from dead works and causes me to serve the living God.

☐ I agree ☐ I disagree ☐ I'm working on it

By the Power of the Stripes of Jesus I am Healed

But he was wounded for our transgressions, he was bruised for our iniquities: the chastisement of our peace was upon him; and with his stripes we are healed.

—Isaiah 53:5

Daily Agreement:
I agree, the power of His stripes heals me.

| ☐ I agree | ☐ I disagree | ☐ I'm working on it |

Using the Word of God is Powerful—
It is Sharper than Any Double-Edge Sword

For the word of God is living and active, sharper than any two-edged sword, piercing to the division of soul and of spirit, of joints and of marrow, and discerning the thoughts and intentions of the heart.

—Hebrews 4:12 ESV

Daily Agreement:
I agree, God's Word is powerful, quick, and sharper than any two-edged sword.

| ☐ I agree | ☐ I disagree | ☐ I'm working on it |

Through God's Divine Power, I Have All Things Pertaining to Life and Godliness

According as his divine power hath given unto us all things that pertain unto life and godliness, through the knowledge of him that hath called us to glory and virtue.

—2 Peter 1:3

Daily Agreement:
I agree through the knowledge of God and his divine power, I have all things pertaining to life and godliness.

| ☐ I agree | ☐ I disagree | ☐ I'm working on it |

Week Nine

Heroine of Power: Elizabeth	103
Day 1: My Words Have Power to Both Justify and Condemn	104
Day 2: We Have the Authority to Remain Steadfast, Unmovable, and Always Abound in the Work of the Lord Through Jesus Christ	105
Day 3: I Have the Power to be Transformed and Not Conformed to This World	106
Day 4: Repent and Be Baptized in the Name of Jesus, then You Will Receive the Gift of the Holy Ghost (Power)!	107
Day 5: I Have the Power to Receive Good Things from My Father	108
Day 6: The Power of the Spirit of God Within Us Makes Intercession and Helps Our Infirmities	109
Day 7: We Have Authority to Live, Move, and Exist in Jesus	110

Heroine of Power: Elizabeth

Power/Authority:
Elizabeth experienced the power of grace in her life.

Purpose/Why:
To carry and deliver a promised child after her childbearing years, the forerunner of Jesus Christ, John the Baptist (Luke 1:13).

Do you agree this power and/or authority is still actively available for use today?

| ☐ I agree | ☐ I disagree | ☐ I'm working on it |

My Words Have Power to Both Justify and Condemn

For by thy words thou shalt be justified, and by thy words thou shalt be condemned.

—Matthew 12:37

Daily Agreement:
I agree, my words will justify or condemn me.

☐ I agree   ☐ I disagree   ☐ I'm working on it

We Have the Authority to Remain Steadfast, Unmovable, and Always Abound in the Work of the Lord Through Jesus Christ

But thanks be to God, which giveth us the victory through our Lord Jesus Christ. Therefore, my beloved brethren, be ye stedfast, unmoveable, always abounding in the work of the Lord, forasmuch as ye know that your labour is not in vain in the Lord.

—1 Corinthians 15:57–58

Daily Agreement:
I agree, I have the victory through Jesus Christ to always abound in the work of the Lord.

| ☐ I agree | ☐ I disagree | ☐ I'm working on it |

I Have the Power to be Transformed and Not Conformed to This World

And be not conformed to this world: but be ye transformed by the renewing of your mind, that ye may prove what is that good, and acceptable, and perfect, will of God.

—Romans 12:2

Daily Agreement:
I agree to be transformed by the renewing of my mind.

| ☐ I agree | ☐ I disagree | ☐ I'm working on it |

Repent and Be Baptized in the Name of Jesus, then You Will Receive the Gift of Holy Ghost (Power)!

Then Peter said unto them, Repent, and be baptized every one of you in the name of Jesus Christ for the remission of sins, and ye shall receive the gift of the Holy Ghost.

—Acts 2:38

Daily Agreement:
I agree, after repentance and baptism in the name of Jesus, then I will receive power.

| ☐ I agree | ☐ I disagree | ☐ I'm working on it |

I Have the Power to Receive Good Things from My Father

If ye then, being evil, know how to give good gifts unto your children, how much more shall your Father which is in heaven give good things to them that ask him?

—Matthew 7:11

Daily Agreement:
I agree, I have the authority to receive good things from the Father when I ask.

| ☐ I agree | ☐ I disagree | ☐ I'm working on it |

The Power of the Spirit of God Within Us Makes Intercession and Helps Our Infirmities

Likewise the Spirit also helpeth our infirmities: for we know not what we should pray for as we ought: but the Spirit itself maketh intercession for us with groanings which cannot be uttered.

—Romans 8:26

Daily Agreement:
I agree, the Spirit of God intercedes on my behalf and helps my infirmities.

| ☐ I agree | ☐ I disagree | ☐ I'm working on it |

We Have Authority to Live, Move, and Exist in Jesus

For in him we live, and move, and have our being; as certain also of your own poets have said, for we are also his offspring.

—Acts 17:28

Daily Agreement:
I agree that I have authority to live, move, and have my being in Jesus.

| ☐ I agree | ☐ I disagree | ☐ I'm working on it |

Week Ten

Hero of Power: David	113
Day 1: By the Power of Faith, I Can Obtain a Good Report	114
Day 2: The Power of Faith Causes My Prayers to be Answered	115
Day 3: I Have the Power to Walk By Faith and Not By What I See	116
Day 4: From the Beginning, God, Who is All Powerful, Made All Things	117
Day 5: I Have Been Given the Power of Grace	118
Day 6: I Have the Power to Fight the Good Fight of Faith	119
Day 7: I Have the Power to Have Good Success	120

Hero of Power: David

Power/Authority:
David used the power of courage to defeat the giant Goliath (1 Samuel 17).

Purpose/Why:
To prove that God's power is greater than human strength.

Do you agree this power and/or authority is still actively available for use today?

| ☐ I agree | ☐ I disagree | ☐ I'm working on it |

By the Power of Faith, I Can Obtain a Good Report

Now faith is the substance of things hoped for, the evidence of things not seen. For by it the elders obtained a good report.

—Hebrews 11:1–2

Daily Agreement:
I agree, the power of faith gives me a good report.

| ☐ I agree | ☐ I disagree | ☐ I'm working on it |

The Power of Faith
Causes My Prayers to be Answered

"… And whatever you ask in prayer, you will receive, if you have faith."

—Matthew 21:22 ESV

Daily Agreement:
I agree, I have whatever I ask in prayer by the power of faith.

| ☐ I agree | ☐ I disagree | ☐ I'm working on it |

I Have the Power to Walk By Faith and Not By What I See

… for we walk by faith, not by sight.
—2 Corinthians 5:7 ESV

Daily Agreement:
I agree, I have power to walk by faith.

| ☐ I agree | ☐ I disagree | ☐ I'm working on it |

From the Beginning, God, Who is All Powerful, Made All Things

In the beginning was the Word, and the Word was with God, and the Word was God. The same was in the beginning with God. All things were made by him; and without him was not any thing made that was made.

—John 1:1–3

Daily Agreement:
I agree, God made all things from the beginning.

| ☐ I agree | ☐ I disagree | ☐ I'm working on it |

I Have Been Given the Power of Grace

But unto every one of us is given grace according to the measure of the gift of Christ.

—Ephesians 4:7

Daily Agreement:
I agree through Christ, I have the power of grace.

| ☐ I agree | ☐ I disagree | ☐ I'm working on it |

I Have the Power to Fight the Good Fight of Faith

But thou, O man of God, flee these things; and follow after righteousness, godliness, faith, love, patience, meekness. Fight the good fight of faith, lay hold on eternal life, whereunto thou art also called, and hast professed a good profession before many witnesses.

—1 Timothy 6:11–12

Daily Agreement:
I agree, I have the power to fight the good fight of faith and lay hold on eternal life.

| ☐ I agree | ☐ I disagree | ☐ I'm working on it |

I Have the Power to Have Good Success

This Book of the Law shall not depart from your mouth, but you shall meditate on it day and night, so that you may be careful to do according to all that is written in it. For then you will make your way prosperous, and then you will have good success. Have I not commanded you? Be strong and courageous. Do not be frightened, and do not be dismayed, for the Lord your God is with you wherever you go."

—Joshua 1:8–9 ESV

Daily Agreement:
I agree, I have the power to create good success through obedience and meditation of the Word of God.

| ☐ I agree | ☐ I disagree | ☐ I'm working on it |

Week Eleven

Heroine of Power: Mary   123
Day 1: I Have Authority Over My Mouth
    Not to Speak Corrupt Communication   124
Day 2: I Have the Power to Forgive
    Just as Christ Forgave Me   125
Day 3: Through the Spirit of Christ, My Body Has Power
    to Be Quickened (to Make Alive)   126
Day 4: I Agree I Have Power Over Sin By Grace   127
Day 5: God's Authority Gives Me a Way of Escape
    During Temptation   128
Day 6: Jesus Has the Keys (Authority)
    Over Death and Hell   129
Day 7: I Have Power Even in My Weakness   130

Heroine of Power: Mary

Power/Authority:
Mary used the power of agreement with God.

Purpose/Why:
To carry and deliver baby Jesus who was conceived by Holy Spirit to bring salvation into the earth.

Do you agree this power and/or authority is still actively available for use today?

| ☐ I agree | ☐ I disagree | ☐ I'm working on it |

I Have Authority Over My Mouth Not to Speak Corrupt Communication

Let no corrupt communication proceed out of your mouth, but that which is good to the use of edifying, that it may minister grace unto the hearers.

—Ephesians 4:29

Daily Agreement:
I agree, my communication will be good, give grace, and edify.

| ☐ I agree | ☐ I disagree | ☐ I'm working on it |

I Have the Power to Forgive
Just as Christ Forgave Me

Be kind to one another, tenderhearted, forgiving one another, as God in Christ forgave you.

—Ephesians 4:32 ESV

Daily Agreement:
I agree, I have forgiveness power.

| ☐ I agree | ☐ I disagree | ☐ I'm working on it |

Through the Spirit of Christ, My Body Has Power to Be Quickened (to Make Alive)

But if Christ is in you, although the body is dead because of sin, the Spirit is life because of righteousness. If the Spirit of him who raised Jesus from the dead dwells in you, he who raised Christ Jesus from the dead will also give life to your mortal bodies through his Spirit who dwells in you.

—Romans 8:10–11 ESV

Daily Agreement:
I agree, I have power to be made alive through the Spirit of Christ.

| ☐ I agree | ☐ I disagree | ☐ I'm working on it |

I Agree I Have Power Over Sin By Grace

For sin shall not have dominion over you: for ye are not under the law, but under grace.

—Romans 6:14

Daily Agreement:
I agree by grace, I can overpower sin.

☐ I agree ☐ I disagree ☐ I'm working on it

God's Authority Gives Me a Way of Escape During Temptation

There hath no temptation taken you but such as is common to man: but God is faithful, who will not suffer you to be tempted above that ye are able; but will with the temptation also make a way to escape, that ye may be able to bear it.

—1 Corinthians 10:13

Daily Agreement:
I agree, I have a way of escape when I am tempted.

| ☐ I agree | ☐ I disagree | ☐ I'm working on it |

Jesus Has the Keys (Authority) Over Death and Hell

I am he that liveth, and was dead; and, behold, I am alive for evermore, Amen; and have the keys of hell and of death.

—Revelation 1:18

Daily Agreement:
I agree, Jesus lived, died, and is living forevermore with authority over death and hell.

| ☐ I agree | ☐ I disagree | ☐ I'm working on it |

I Have Power Even in My Weakness

And he said unto me, My grace is sufficient for thee: for my strength is made perfect in weakness. Most gladly therefore will I rather glory in my infirmities, that the power of Christ may rest upon me.

—2 Corinthians 12:9

Daily Agreement:
I agree through the grace of Jesus, my strength is made perfect in weakness.

| ☐ I agree | ☐ I disagree | ☐ I'm working on it |

Week Twelve

Hero of Power: John the Baptist	133
Day 1: Because God Will Not Fail, I Have the Power to Be Strong and Courageous	134
Day 2: I Have the Power to Judge Righteously	135
Day 3: I Have the Power to Discern True and False	136
Day 4: Through the Power of Jesus Christ, I Have the Power to Wrestle Against Evil Powers, Rulers of Darkness, and Against Spiritual Wickedness in High Places	137
Day 5: Dressed in the Full Armor of God, I Have the Power to Stand Against the Wiles of the Devil	138
Day 6: Each Piece of My Armor Serves a Purpose to Help Me Withstand in the Evil Day	139
Day 7: I Have Unstoppable Praying Power	140

Hero of Power: John the Baptist

Power/Authority:

John used the authority of water baptism unto repentance.

Purpose/Why:

To prepare the way for Jesus who would baptize with the fire of the Holy Spirit.

Do you agree this power and/or authority is still actively available for use today?

| ☐ I agree | ☐ I disagree | ☐ I'm working on it |

Because God Will Not Fail, I Have the Power to Be Strong and Courageous

Be strong and of a good courage, fear not, nor be afraid of them: for the Lord thy God, he it is that doth go with thee; he will not fail thee, nor forsake thee.

—Deuteronomy 31:6

Daily Agreement:
I agree, I have the power to be fearless because God will not fail me.

☐ I agree   ☐ I disagree   ☐ I'm working on it

I Have the Power to Judge Righteously

Judge not according to the appearance but judge righteous judgment.

—John 7:24

Daily Agreement:
I agree that righteous judgement is within my authority.

| ☐ I agree | ☐ I disagree | ☐ I'm working on it |

I Have the Power to Discern True and False

If anyone's will is to do God's will, he will know whether the teaching is from God or whether I am speaking on my own authority. The one who speaks on his own authority seeks his own glory; but the one who seeks the glory of him who sent him is true, and in him there is no falsehood.
—John 7:17–18 ESV

Daily Agreement:
I agree, I have the power to know the difference between truth and falsehood.

| ☐ I agree | ☐ I disagree | ☐ I'm working on it |

Through the Power of Jesus Christ, I Have the Power to Wrestle Against Evil Powers, Rulers of Darkness, and Against Spiritual Wickedness in High Places

For we wrestle not against flesh and blood, but against principalities, against powers, against the rulers of the darkness of this world, against spiritual wickedness in high places.

—Ephesians 6:12

Daily Agreement:
I agree through Jesus, I have the power to fight against spiritual wickedness in high places.

| ☐ I agree | ☐ I disagree | ☐ I'm working on it |

Dressed in the Full Armor of God, I Have the Power to Stand Against the Wiles of the Devil

Put on the whole armour of God, that ye may be able to stand against the wiles of the devil.

—Ephesians 6:11

Daily Agreement:
I agree, the armor of God protects me from the wiles of the enemy.

| ☐ I agree | ☐ I disagree | ☐ I'm working on it |

Each Piece of My Armor Serves a Purpose to Help Me Withstand in the Evil Day

Wherefore take unto you the whole armour of God, that ye may be able to withstand in the evil day, and having done all, to stand. Stand therefore, having your loins girt about with truth, and having on the breastplate of righteousness; And your feet shod with the preparation of the gospel of peace; Above all, taking the shield of faith, wherewith ye shall be able to quench all the fiery darts of the wicked. And take the helmet of salvation, and the sword of the Spirit, which is the word of God.

—Ephesians 6:13–17

Daily Agreement:
I agree, after doing all to stand, I will stand clothed in every piece of God's armor.

| ☐ I agree | ☐ I disagree | ☐ I'm working on it |

I Have Unstoppable Praying Power

Pray without ceasing.

—1 Thessalonians 5:17

Daily Agreement:
I agree, I have the power to pray without ceasing.

| ☐ I agree | ☐ I disagree | ☐ I'm working on it |

Week Thirteen

Hero of Power: Abraham — 142

Day 1: I Shall Not Die, but Live! — 144

Day 2: Through Jesus, I Have the Authority to Bind and Loose in Heaven and in Earth — 145

Day 3: Through the Lord, I Have a Powerful Heritage and No Weapon Formed Against Me Will Prosper — 146

Day 4: God Gives Me the Power of Understanding to Know the True God and to Stay Away from Idols — 147

Day 5: I Have Powerful Weapons of Warfare with Divine Power to Destroy Thought Strongholds — 148

Day 6: Through Jesus, I Have the Power of Agreement to Receive What I Ask — 149

Day 7: Through Jesus I Have Power to Do Greater Works — 150

Hero of Power: Abraham

Power/Authority:
Abraham used the power of agreement in covenant faith to receive the promises of God.

Purpose/Why:
God used Abraham because Abraham believed God. He trusted and obeyed God. His belief in the Lord was counted unto him as righteousness. Therefore, his name was changed from Abram to Abraham and he became the father unto many nations (Genesis 15–17).

Do you agree this power and/or authority is still actively available for use today?

| ☐ I agree | ☐ I disagree | ☐ I'm working on it |

I Shall Not Die, but Live!

Ye are of God, little children, and have overcome them: because greater is he that is in you, than he that is in the world.
—Psalm 118:17

Daily Agreement:
I agree, I shall not die, but live and declare the salvation of the Lord!

☐ I agree   ☐ I disagree   ☐ I'm working on it

Through Jesus, I Have the Authority to Bind and Loose in Heaven and in Earth

Verily I say unto you, Whatsoever ye shall bind on earth shall be bound in heaven: and whatsoever ye shall loose on earth shall be loosed in heaven.

—Matthew 18:18

Daily Agreement:
I agree through Jesus, I have binding and loosing authority in heaven and earth.

☐ I agree ☐ I disagree ☐ I'm working on it

Through the Lord, I Have a Powerful Heritage and No Weapon Formed Against Me Will Prosper

No weapon that is formed against thee shall prosper; and every tongue that shall rise against thee in judgment thou shalt condemn. This is the heritage of the servants of the Lord, and their righteousness is of me, saith the Lord.
—Isaiah 54:17

Daily Agreement:
I agree, I am a servant of the Lord and I have a powerful inheritance in which no weapon formed against me will prosper and every tongue risen against me in judgment, the Lord will condemn.

☐ I agree	☐ I disagree	☐ I'm working on it

God Gives Me the Power of Understanding to Know the True God and to Stay Away from Idols

And we know that the Son of God is come, and hath given us an understanding, that we may know him that is true, and we are in him that is true, even in his Son Jesus Christ. This is the true God, and eternal life. Little children, keep yourselves from idols. Amen.

—1 John 5:20–21

Daily Agreement:
I agree that through the power of understanding Him that is true, I will stay away from idols.

| ☐ I agree | ☐ I disagree | ☐ I'm working on it |

I Have Powerful Weapons of Warfare with Divine Power to Destroy Thought Strongholds

For the weapons of our warfare are not of the flesh but have divine power to destroy strongholds. We destroy arguments and every lofty opinion raised against the knowledge of God, and take every thought captive to obey Christ,

—2 Corinthians 10:4–5 ESV

Daily Agreement:
I agree, I have divine power to bring my thoughts captive and obey Christ.

| ☐ I agree | ☐ I disagree | ☐ I'm working on it |

Through Jesus, I Have the Power of Agreement to Receive What I Ask

Again I say unto you, That if two of you shall agree on earth as touching any thing that they shall ask, it shall be done for them of my Father which is in heaven. For where two or three are gathered together in my name, there am I in the midst of them.

—Matthew 18:19–20

Daily Agreement:
I agree, if two of us agree on earth about anything we ask, it will be done for us by my Father in heaven.

| ☐ I agree | ☐ I disagree | ☐ I'm working on it |

Through Jesus I Have Power to Do Greater Works

Believe me that I am in the Father and the Father is in me, or else believe on account of the works themselves. "Truly, truly, I say to you, whoever believes in me will also do the works that I do; and greater works than these will he do, because I am going to the Father. Whatever you ask in my name, this I will do, that the Father may be glorified in the Son.
—John 14:11–13 ESV

Daily Agreement:
I agree, Jesus gives me authority to do the same and greater works because He went to the Father.

☐ I agree   ☐ I disagree   ☐ I'm working on it

About the Author

Bobbie Goodwin loves the Lord Jesus. She has been happily married since 2010. She has three loving and inspiring adult children and eight blessed grandchildren.

Born in Iowa, but grew up in Memphis, Tennessee, Bobbie graduated from Treadwell High School. She obtained her bachelor's degree from Union University. She is currently completing her MBA degree at Union University.

She loves to empower and encourage others. Bobbie loves to laugh and spend time with family and friends. Traveling the world, embracing new opportunities, and teaching the Word of God are also some of her favorite moments.

Agree.

Made in the USA
Columbia, SC
07 December 2024